GARLIC FOR HEALTH

by
BENJAMIN LAU, M.D., Ph.D.

613. 26
+ 6⁰⁰s

1. Diseases — Prevention
2. Heart — Diseases — Prevention
3. Garlic — medicinal uses
I T

Printed in Japan
Library of Congress Catalog Card Number 88-80886
ISBN 0-941524-32-9

From the Publisher:

This book does not intend to diagnose disease nor to provide
specific medical advice. Its intention is solely to inform and to
educate. The author and publisher intend that readers will use
the information presented in this book in cooperation with a
medical or health professional.

CONTENTS

ACKNOWLEDGEMENTS

Writing this book was a family project—partly because much of it was written when my family and I were on "vacation" in some secluded area away from the noise of my busy laboratory, the constant visits from students and colleagues, and the seemingly endless telephone calls. I am very fortunate to have a wife and two children who tolerate my terrible habit of combining work and leisure—without them, I could not have written these pages.

It was a family project in other ways, too. My two children, Daniel and Shari, volunteered much of their free time to type, edit, and retype my manuscript.

Others had an invaluable hand in this project as well. I thank my very competent technician, Kiok Lim, who patiently assisted in many of the tests described in this book. Former and current graduate students provided a constant source of inspiration, energy, and curiosity; they include Moses Adetumbi, Gregory Kuo, Mary LaBue, Jeff Tosk and Padma Tadi. I am so thankful that each of them shared a part of their very productive lives with me.

I also want to thank my medical colleagues for their untiring efforts in my lab helping to refine various research projects; they include Christopher Marsh, Gary Barker, Craig Myers, James Woolley, and Dale Kunihira.

I thank my two sisters-in-law, Becky Wang-Cheng and Ruth Liu who provided invaluable suggestions for improving this manuscript.

And last, but definitely not least, I thank Bill and Judy Khoe, who have for more than a decade shared with me their ideas and inspiration on many subjects.

GARLIC AND MODERN MEDICINE

We are living in an exciting time of enhanced health awareness. Manufacturers are constantly putting out new products and services promising better health. A casual glance through a typical newspaper tells the story. On one page is an eye-catching ad for a health spa. Crossing over, we find an ad for diet pills promising no harmful side effects. Continuing our search, we find a page advertising a popular exercise home video.

There are subtle health messages, too, coming at us from packages, grocery store aisles, and television screens. The Surgeon General's warnings on cigarette packages and on glossy magazine pages remind us that there's a price to pay for lighting up. Consumers in increasing numbers are responding to nutrition information by becoming vegetarians. Even commercials for sugar explain why it's not that bad for you!

In all the mania about health, a small cloved vegetable—*Allium sativum*, or garlic as we better know it—has been largely neglected. Why? Maybe because of its long association with superstition and folk medicine. After all, ancient civilizations believed that demons caused disease. To get rid of the demons, they ate garlic.

Or maybe garlic has been ignored as a medicinal food because of its strong odor—and the social problems that inevitably follow.

Or it might be that few are aware of exactly what garlic has to offer: with all the well-publicized work being done on a variety of diseases, garlic hasn't exactly made front-page news.

The fact is that growing numbers of well-respected scientists are quietly unlocking an expanding knowledge of garlic's benefits. Many in Japan and elsewhere have even discovered how to develop a product that retains all of garlic's healthful properties—without its pungent odor. Simply stated, garlic is no longer just an ingredient in the anecdotes of folk medicine.

Only a few years ago, I too thought garlic belonged to the realm of folklore and doubted those who even suggested medicinal value for this herb. However, at last glance, I was surprised to note that more than one thousand scientific papers have been published about the various aspects of *Allium*, most of them within the past fifteen years. Several excellent review articles have also been published. For example, Drs. Fenwick and Hanley from the United Kingdom published a three-part comprehensive review of nutritional and medicinal aspects of the genus *Allium* in *Critical Reviews in Food Science and Nutrition* (1,2,3). Another equally extensive thesis by these same authors was published in the *Journal of Plant Foods* (4). American researcher Dr. Eric Block, Professor of Chemistry at the State University of New York in Albany, published a landmark article on garlic and onions in *Scientific American* (5) which has generated a lot of interest among scientists as well as the general public.

In the pages that follow, I would like to share with you some important findings made by modern scientists on the potential benefits of garlic on allergies, high blood pressure, cancer, fungal and viral infections, cardiovascular disease, stress, immunity, and more. But first, let me tell you how I became interested in garlic. . .

2

THE BEGINNINGS
OF OUR GARLIC RESEARCH

My first taste of garlic research came several years ago when a physician friend mentioned in casual conversation that he had used garlic preparations in his practice—and that his patients had enjoyed relief from a variety of complaints. I had great respect for this colleague as he was (and still is) a very successful practitioner and had published a great deal of medical literature, so I was baffled as to why a man of his caliber was using folk remedies in this modern day and age. In the course of our conversation, he mentioned that garlic is a potent antibiotic and inhibitor of many microorganisms. As a professor of microbiology, I began devising in my mind a test to find out if my friend was right.

At the time, my students and I were doing experiments testing the ability of various potent drugs to stop the growth of different bacteria and fungi. Upon returning to my laboratory, I prepared diluted garlic extract, introduced it to several of the cultures, and stuck them in the incubator overnight. The next day I was astounded to find that the diluted garlic extract did indeed stop the growth of those cultures, more effectively, in fact, than some of the potent drugs we were testing at the time.

I shared the finding with my Ph.D. student, Moses Adetumbi, who immediately went to the library to check out the literature. He found that a number of papers had already been published by microbiologists and other researchers, showing garlic to be a potent, broad-spectrum antibiotic. After several days in the library copying papers, Moses and I began carefully scrutinizing what had been written about garlic.

We found interest to be broad and research to be fascinating. There were papers written by Indian, Japanese, and European researchers—as well as some extensive and well-documented studies by American investigators. Dr. Carl Fliermans, for example, did a study at the University of Kentucky in Lexington showing that garlic inhibited *Histoplasma capsulatum*, an important fungal pathogen in that part of the country (6). I was a graduate student at the University of Kentucky at that time but was somehow unaware of his research. Dr. Michael R. Tansey and his associates at Indiana University, Bloomington, did a series of studies on garlic's effect on large numbers of molds and yeasts (7,8,9). Dr. Robert A. Fromtling (now with Merck Institute for Therapeutic Research, Rahway, New Jersey) did his work at the University of Oklahoma showing garlic inhibited the growth of *Cryptococcus neoformans*, a yeast organism responsible for some serious meningitis (10). Dr. Edward Delaha and Vincent Garagusi of George Washington University, Washington D.C. showed garlic inhibited the growth of many acid-fast bacteria including species causing tuberculosis (11). There were many more interesting papers, and I was embarrassed for being ignorant of these reports. The only rationale I could give to justify myself was that we researchers are too busy with our own work and thus have no time to get involved with subjects not directly related. This is the price we pay for being super-specialists. The lesson to be learned of course is not to be close-minded and judgmental on subjects one is not well-acquainted with.

Moses, originally from Nigeria, had wanted to conduct research that would be meaningful to his country and that he could continue when he returned to his homeland. With some persuasion, he convinced me to guide him on a research project to find out how garlic exerts its antimicrobial property using modern technology available in our laboratory. And so began our garlic research.

Moses began his study with 30 pounds of Schilling instant garlic powder donated to us by McCormick Company of Gilroy, California. He showed that an extract of garlic powder inhibits the growth of a variety of microorganisms. He worked particularly with *Coccidioides immitis* (12), a mold that causes Valley Fever throughout the western United States, and *Candida albicans* (13), a yeast organism that has received a lot of publicity in recent years. Moses found that garlic acts on the lipid layer of the membrane, interfering with lipid synthesis (see Figure 1) and with the yeast organism's ability to take up oxygen (see Figure 3). It did not, however, affect the synthesis of protein or nucleic acids (see Figure 2). In other words, garlic causes these microbes to lose their membrane, the lining of their bodies, and consequently they can no longer breathe.

Moses presented his findings at scientific meetings, and his reports were very well received. Dr. Tansey of Indiana University came to some of these meetings and encouraged Moses to continue this line of research. Several newspapers described our work, and we published three papers on this subject as a part of his Ph.D. work (12,13,14). Moses is now teaching in Nigeria and is still involved with garlic research.

While most studies, including our own, were done in vitro or in test tubes because of the ease of such experiments, there were also quite a number of studies done with animals. For example, Drs. Prasad and Sharma in India were able to control *Candida albicans* infection in chicks with oral feeding of garlic (15). Studies conducted in Egypt demonstrated the ability of garlic extract to cure

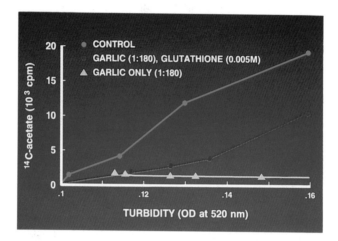

Figure 1. Lipid biosynthesis by *Candida albicans* in the
control culture, culture containing garlic, and culture
containing garlic pretreated with glutathione. Radioactivity in the chloroform-methanol extract of each 0.8 ml
sample was used to estimate lipid synthesis. The graph
shows control without garlic (blue circle) had an
increase of lipid synthesis reflected by increased uptake
of ¹⁴C-acetate whereas in the presence of garlic (triangle), no lipid synthesis was noted. Glutathione, a sulfhydryl compound, reduced some of the inhibition. OD,
Optical density. From (13) with permission.

ringworm infection in rabbits (16).

What about human studies? Researchers at Hunan
Medical College in the People's Republic of China used
garlic to successfully treat eleven victims of meningitis
caused by *Cryptococcus neoformans* (17). Over a period
of several weeks, garlic extract was administered orally
and also, intramuscularly or intravenously. Side effects
were minimal, including transient chills, low grade fever,
headache, nausea, vomiting and pain at the site of injec-

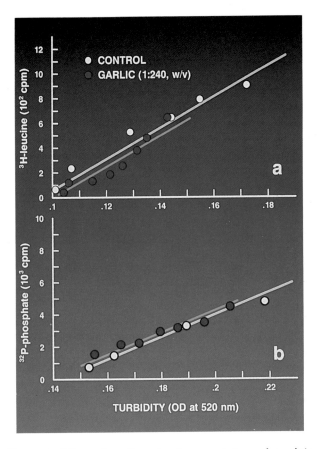

Figure 2. Effect of garlic extract on protein and nucleic acid biosyntheses in *Candida albicans*. (a) [³H]leucine was incorporated into cold acid-insoluble fractions to estimate the amount of protein synthesis in the presence or absence of garlic extract. (b) [³²P]phosphate was incorporated into a hot acid-soluble fraction to determine the amount of nucleic acid synthesis in the presence or absence of garlic. Samples in both experiments were taken at 15 minute intervals. The graphs show that garlic extract did not affect the biosynthesis of these macromolecules. OD, Optical density. From (13) with permission.

tion. Obviously, the Chinese were quite daring to conduct such an experiment. This type of meningitis was also treated by physicians in Singapore using garlic along with conventional antifungal drugs (18).

Researchers in India used garlic with success against sporotrichosis, a stubborn fungal infection of the soft tissues and lymphatics usually transmitted from contaminated roses or other thorny plants. Garlic extract applied over the ulcerated tissue cleared the infection (19).

Aside from mold and yeast-related problems, my colleagues and I are now seeing a lot of patients with chronic viral infections such as syndromes related to Epstein-Barr virus, cytomegalovirus and herpes simplex virus. Several studies have shown that garlic inhibits viral multiplication. For example, Dr. Yen Tsai from the Shanghai Second Medical College, People's Republic of China, collaborating with scientists at the University of New Mexico Medical School recently reported that garlic has antiviral activity against influenza virus and herpes simplex virus (20). Two other studies, one by Japanese (21) and the other by Romanian (22) researchers showed that garlic extract reduced the severity of influenza virus infection in mice. Garlic was also shown to potentiate the antibody response in animals immunized with an influenza vaccine (21). Recently, a medical student working with me found that human immunodeficiency virus (HIV) or AIDS virus did not grow well in the presence of garlic in tissue culture. The possibilities seemed staggering!

Worldwide research continues to show the vast properties of garlic. A colleague of mine doing leprosy research sent me a reprint not long ago showing garlic was successfully used in India for treating leprosy (23). A Tufts University medical student doing summer research at Israel's Weizmann Institute found that garlic stopped the growth of *Entamoeba histolytica*, the parasite that causes nearly 400 million cases of dysentery diarrhea in the world each year (24). Interestingly, the Tufts University student heard about garlic's curative properties from a Peace Corps volunteer—but no one at Tufts was aware of garlic as a remedy.

Apparently garlic does have a very broad range of activity against a variety of microorganisms. Dr. Adetumbi and I wrote a paper a few years ago in *Medical Hypotheses* (14) reviewing this subject. Since then, more papers have appeared in the literature confirming the effectiveness of garlic against viruses, bacteria, spirochetes, molds, yeasts, and parasites.

Scientists are now interested in finding out which components of garlic exert its antimicrobial activity. For years we thought that allicin, the part that gives garlic its pungent odor, was the main component. But, recent research by Dr. Nakagawa and his associates in Japan showed that ajoene, a component isolated by Dr. Eric Block and associates in New York (25), is superior to allicin in antifungal activity (26).

Meanwhile, many physicians and patients tell us that they have fewer colds and recover faster from viral infections as a result of garlic supplementation. Our own research left us with little doubt that components of garlic indeed have pharmacologic and therapeutic properties.

But what about the odor? In our review of the literature, we noted that in India or China, test subjects took one ounce or more of garlic every day throughout the study. Would Americans be willing to do this? Obviously, odor was a stumbling block. My associates and I then began to look into various odor-modified garlic preparations. . . .

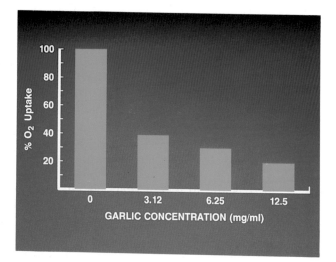

Figure 3. The uptake of oxygen by a yeast culture *Candida albicans* was measured by a Clark oxygen electrode attached to Model 53 Biological Oxygen Monitor and a Curken Model 250 recorder. Inhibition of oxygen uptake in the presence of garlic extract is dose-related as shown in the figure.

△3

ODOR-MODIFIED GARLIC

We discovered from several physicians who were using garlic in their practice that Wakunaga Pharmaceutical in Japan had been manufacturing "sociable odorless garlic" for more than twenty years. This pharmaceutical firm's research center, comprised more than 20 Ph.D.'s, M.D.'s, and D.V.M.'s, has done research on garlic and other herbal medicine since 1954. They have published extensively in Japanese journals and in recent years also in English. In the last few years, companies in the United States and elsewhere have also begun making odor-modified garlic preparations.

While Moses Adetumbi concentrated his study on antimicrobial properties, I became interested in the effect of garlic on regulating lipid metabolism. I noted that nearly all the studies in both animals and humans employed either fresh garlic juice or essential oil extracted from garlic with the belief that the odorous components of garlic such as allicin are needed to regulate lipids. We then found two reports by Dr. Asaf A. Qureshi, research chemist with Barley and Malt Laboratory, U.S. Department of Agriculture (27,28). In these papers, the researchers evaluated different fractions of garlic extract in chickens and reported that the odorless water-soluble component of garlic was equally effective in lowering blood cholesterol and triglycerides.

In collaboration with two internist colleagues, we decided to conduct a clinical study on blood lipids with Kyolic, an "odorless garlic" product from Japan; study results were published in *Nutrition Research* (29).

The first part of the three-part study involved thirty-two subjects with elevated levels of cholesterol (220-440 mg/dl), randomly divided into two groups. The first group received four capsules a day of liquid Kyolic garlic extract. Members of the other group received four capsules of a placebo—a caramel-colored solution indistinguishable from the Kyolic garlic extract.

Blood lipids were measured each month. Those who took the placebo showed no significant change. But imagine our dismay when we found that those taking the Kyolic had actually experienced an increase in serum cholesterol and triglycerides in the first two months!

We were ready to abandon our research when we found that researchers using fresh garlic had encountered the same results in the first few months. Indian researcher Dr. Arun Bordia, studying patients with coronary heart disease, found that garlic supplementation initially raised serum lipids (see Figure 4). He postulated that garlic moves lipids from where they have been deposited in the tissues, depositing them instead in the bloodstream (30). Researchers at the United States Department of Agriculture's Nutrition Institute found the same thing: rats fed garlic extract for eighteen days had fewer lipid deposits in the liver but higher serum lipids (see Table 1) (31).

Table 1. Effect of garlic on tissue and blood lipids*

	Fat diet	Fat & Garlic
Liver total lipid (mg/dg)	552	338
Liver cholesterol (mg/dg)	60	42
Serum cholesterol (mg/dg)	198	208
Serum triglyceride (mg/dg)	386	454

* Rats were on diet for 18 days. Adapted from (31) with permission.

Buoyed by these findings, we continued our study. Beginning in the third month, we saw a significant drop in serum lipids; they reached a low level—approaching normal values—at <u>six</u> months. The result? We believe based on our research that garlic causes lipid deposits to shift into the bloodstream, causing initially higher serum lipid levels; subsequently, with continued garlic, excess serum lipids are broken down and excreted through the intestinal tract. Several independent studies have reported that this actually occurs in animals who are fed garlic (32,33,34,35).

In the second part of the study, fourteen subjects with a normal range of serum lipids were randomly divided into two groups: the first received Kyolic, and the second a placebo. We repeated our method. We were not surprised to find that lipid parameters in both groups went virtually unchanged by the end of the study. Interestingly, however, among those who took Kyolic there was a modest rise in cholesterol and triglycerides during the first two months—presumably as garlic mobilized lipid deposits from the tissues to the extracellular fluid.

In the last part of the three-part study, we again used subjects with high blood cholesterol; they were given Kyolic garlic extract for six months. After an initial rise in blood cholesterol and triglycerides, 65 percent experienced a drop in serum lipid levels (see Figure 5).

In this part of the study, we differentiated between low-density lipoproteins, considered to be detrimental to health, and high-density lipoprotein, known to protect against heart attack and stroke. Those taking garlic experienced an initial rise in the level of LDL and VLDL (low-density lipoprotein and very low-density lipoprotein). The initial rise was followed by a significant drop beginning in the third month. As the study progressed, subjects experienced an increase in HDL (high-density

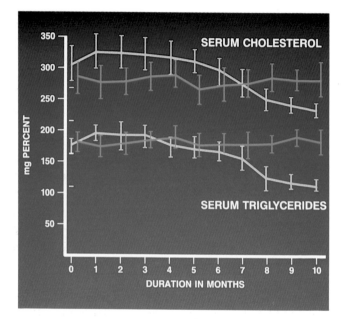

Figure 4. Effect of 10 months of garlic administration on serum cholesterol and triglycerides in patients of coronary heart disease (yellow lines) compared with similar patients without garlic (blue lines). Vertical lines indicate mean ± standard error. Note initial rise of these lipids with garlic administration. From (30) with permission.

lipoprotein) (see Figure 6). In other words, garlic can reduce the levels of "bad" cholesterol while increasing the levels of "good" cholesterol.

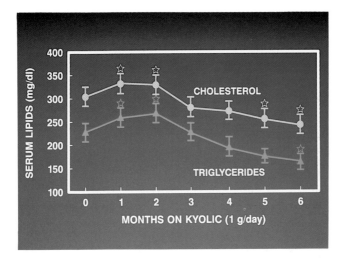

Figure 5. Effect of an odor-modified garlic extract (Kyolic) on blood lipids of human subjects. Each point in the graph represents mean ± standard error. ☆ indicates significantly different from baseline by Tukey's HSD (honestly significant difference) test. Note initial rise of these lipids followed by significant drop below baseline values while subjects took four capsules (4 ml) of Kyolic each day. From (29) with permission.

I mentioned that we were able to observe a significant drop in cholesterol and triglycerides in 65 percent of those taking four capsules a day of Kyolic. What about the other 35 percent who did not respond? Reviewing their dietary history, we discovered that they were heavy meat eaters with diets consisting regularly of steak, pastries, and ice cream, particularly during the evening meals. When we incorporated dietary modification for these individuals, lowering of lipids was then observed in those who were able to follow the recommended dietary changes. Our conclusion is that garlic should be used together with a good diet to achieve the best result. It does not seem likely that one can continue to indulge in all the rich "goodies" and expect a little plant like garlic to protect him. Garlic should, therefore, be used together with a sensible diet.

In 1983, we published a paper in *Nutrition Research* entitled *"Allium sativum* (garlic) and atherosclerosis - a review" (36). Our recent study basically confirmed the findings in the literature and demonstrated that the lipid regulating effect can be achieved with an odorless garlic product.

Why are blood lipids so important?

Coronary artery disease is the number-one killer in America today; cerebrovascular disease is third, surpassed only by cancer. High levels of blood cholesterol and triglycerides are a known risk factor for both.

Here's what happens: Lipids in the bloodstream accumulate and deposit on the walls of blood vessels, causing them to thicken and become narrowed—a process we call atherosclerosis. If the process continues, the blood vessels eventually plug up completely. If the plugged-up vessel is an artery that feeds the heart with blood, the result is a myocardial infarction or heart attack. If the plugged-up vessel is one that feeds the brain, the result is a stroke.

What about "good" cholesterol? Simply stated, the "good" cholesterol (high-density lipoprotein) is much denser and heavier than the low-density lipoprotein. As it circulates in the bloodstream, it is not likely to stick to the walls of blood vessels; in fact, it adheres to the low-density lipoprotein, pulling it away from the blood vessel walls and transporting it to the liver, where it is broken down and excreted from the body (37,38).

Other blood factors—such as the amount of clotting material and the time it takes blood to clot—contribute to heart attack and stroke (39,40), as do factors like high blood pressure, family history, obesity, cigarette smoking, and diabetes mellitus.

How does garlic affect these additional factors?

Blood cells called thrombocytes or platelets normally aggregate or clump together to help prevent blood loss in case of injury; fibrinogen in the blood works with the platelet aggregate through a complicated process to help stop bleeding and to facilitate healing. Without this process, a simple cut could result in fatal blood loss.

A third blood component, plasmin (fibrinolysin), dissolves the fibrin clots when they are no longer needed.

Research has shown that those prone to heart attack and stroke have too much fibrinogen (which causes clots) and not enough fibrinolysin (which breaks up clots). In a chapter outlining the effect of garlic on these factors (41), I explained how garlic prevents the formation of clots. In simple summary, garlic prevents the formation of clots, inhibits platelet aggregation, lowers blood pressure, reduces plaque formation in the arteries, and even reverses established arteriosclerosis.

An epidemiological study of Jain, an Indian community, gives evidence of garlic's impact on the health of the cardiovascular system (42,43,44). Those who take garlic as part of their diet have lower cholesterol, triglycerides, fibrinogen, a longer clotting time, and an increased ability to break up clots when compared to those who do not eat garlic.

Hypertension or high blood pressure is one of the major risk factors of atherosclerosis. It is estimated that more than fifteen percent of the adult population in the United States are hypertensive. Few drugs for controlling

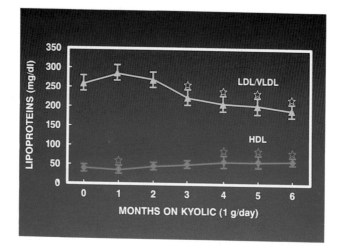

Figure 6. Effect of an odor-modified garlic extract (Kyolic) on blood lipoproteins of human subjects. Each point in the graph represents mean ± standard error. ☆ indicates significantly different from baseline by Tukey's HSD test. Subjects took four Kyolic capsules each day. From (29) with permission.

blood pressure are without side effects. One of the most distressful side effects in the male patients is impotence. These patients become irritable, frustrated and depressed. According to Bolton, Null and Troetel (45), garlic has been used for treating hypertension in China and Japan for centuries and is recognized officially for this purpose by the Japanese Food and Drug administration. Dr. Bolton is a Professor of Pharmacy at St. John's University College of Pharmacy and Allied Health Professions, Jamaica, New York.

As early as 1921, researchers reported the beneficial

effects of garlic in controlling hypertension in both humans and animals (46). In the 1940s, one researcher tested one hundred hypertensive patients by giving them initially large doses of garlic, gradually tapering the amount of garlic as the experiment progressed. He reported that after just one week of garlic treatment, forty of the subjects had a drop of 20 mm Hg or more in their blood pressure (47). Other small-scale studies have shown similar positive effects of garlic on hypertension (48,49).

A recent study by the Chinese Cooperative Group involved seventy hypertensive patients who were given the equivalent of 50 grams of raw garlic a day (50). Thirty-three of the subjects showed a marked lowering of blood pressure; fourteen showed moderate reductions in blood pressure, for an overall success rate of 61.7 percent. Another study conducted at the People's Experimental Academy of Health of Zheziang Province also used essential oil of garlic; that study demonstrated similar results in lowering blood pressure (51).

The Bulgarian researcher Petkov conducted extensive studies involving both animals and humans in an attempt to demonstrate the effects of garlic on high blood pressure (52,53,54,55,56,57). Petkov gave cats intravenous injections of fresh garlic juice; at higher doses, the cats experienced only a slight and temporary decrease in blood pressure. But when the garlic had been prepared and stored for seven to twelve months, the blood pressure-lowering activity was significantly increased. Why? Petkov surmised that storage enabled certain enzyme processes to release the active components of the garlic.

Petkov then tried garlic on twenty-one humans with high blood pressure, using extracts derived from garlic leaves (56). Subjects experienced a systolic pressure drop of 20 to 30 mm Hg and a diastolic pressure drop of 10 to 20 mm Hg. Subjects also noted improvement of other physical symptoms, such as headaches, dizziness, angina-like chest pain, and backaches.

While small-scale studies by independent researchers seem to indicate that garlic is beneficial in controlling blood pressure, large-scale double-blind testing has not yet been—and probably will not be—done. Why? First, garlic is generally classified as an "orphan" drug—one that has therapeutic application but no commercial potential. Without the prospect of financial return, it is not likely that any pharmaceutical concern will undertake the task of conducting a controlled, large-scale investigation.

An additional problem is the fact that blood pressure changes in response to emotional and environmental changes. An Italian hospital study showed how vast these changes can be (58). In the Italian study, forty-eight hospital patients with high or normal blood pressure had their blood pressure monitored electronically by a recorder that was embedded in an artery for a twenty-four-hour period. During that time, patients were free to move around the hospital except for thirty minutes in the morning and afternoon when routine blood pressures were taken with a manual cuff.

A male doctor other than the one assigned to the patients was in charge of taking blood pressures with the manual cuff. The systolic blood pressure rose in all but one patient, and the diastolic rose in all but three patients when the doctor came to take blood pressure readings. The systolic rises ranged from 4 to 75 mm Hg, with a mean of 27; the diastolic rises ranged from 1 to 36, with a mean of 15; peak values were reached within one to four minutes of the doctor's arrival. Obviously, human beings are very sensitive to emotional and environmental influences.

Because diabetes is a risk factor in the development of atherosclerotic disease, it is important to understand the effect of garlic in regulating blood sugar. As early as 1958, Indian researchers showed that blood sugar levels dropped when subjects ate garlic (59). Nearly two decades later, researchers at RNT Medical College in India induced diabetes in rabbits with intravenous injections of alloxan. When fed garlic, the rabbits' elevated blood sugar dropped almost as much as it did when they were given the antidiabetic drug tolbutamide. Researchers postulated that garlic may improve the insulin effect by either increasing the pancreatic secretion of insulin or by releasing bound insulin (60,61).

Additional research bears out the effect of garlic on blood sugar. Researchers at the United States Department of Agriculture showed in a sophisticated study that garlic feeding increased serum insulin levels (31). Another study by Wakunaga Pharmaceutical investigators showed that liquid Kyolic garlic extract prevented the rise of blood sugar after oral loading of glucose in a standard glucose tolerance test (62).

To end this chapter, let me summarize in Table 2 how

Table 2. Summary of lipid regulating and anticoagulant effects of garlic

Garlic decreases	Garlic increases
Cholesterol	HDL
Triglycerides	Fibrinolytic activity
LDL	Blood coagulation time
VLDL	
Plasma fibrinogen	
Platelet aggregation	
Atheromatous lesions	

well garlic fares with various factors in the cardiovascular system:

It is obvious from the table that the influence of garlic on cardiovascular health is vast. Garlic boosts high-density lipoprotein, increases fibrinolytic activity (needed to dissolve clots), and increases blood coagulation time (reducing the risk of clotting disorders). Garlic reduces cholesterol, triglycerides, low density lipoproteins, plasma fibrinogen, platelet aggregation, and plaque on the arterial walls—for overall benefits to cardiovascular health.

But how does garlic help control these blood factors?

In the next chapter, I will discuss with you scientific studies dealing with the question "How garlic affects fat metabolism". ...

△4△

HOW GARLIC REGULATES OUR BLOOD LIPIDS

Many of my health conscious patients would like to keep their blood lipid levels low. They are not satisfied with the American "norm" of 220 mg/dl for cholesterol and would like to keep the level below 200 mg/dl. When they discover that my wife and I have cholesterol levels in the range of 150-160 mg/dl, they want to be more like the Laus and insist that we tell them our secrets. This gives me the occasion to present them with a mini-lecture on the causes of hyperlipidemia or what causes high levels of blood lipids.

Cholesterol, triglycerides, and other fat molecules in our blood are derived from three sources: The first source is our food intake. The more fatty foods we eat, the more fat will be absorbed into our blood. Whatever our body cannot use will be stored in the tissues and spilled over into the blood. When a person is young and active, much of the fat is burned and very little is stored. When a person is older and not so active however, the fat will be stored in the blood and other places such as the belly to produce a "bay window".

The second source of blood lipids is "endogenous lipo-genesis", in other words, the fats made by our body cells. Nearly all of our cells can make fats, but the main manufacturers are the cells in the liver and the adipose tissues (fat pads). The liver can make fats even from simple sugars we eat in our diet.

The third source of blood lipids is not so much of a source, but is rather associated with a lack of fat breakdown and elimination. You see, normally our body will break down fat molecules as a normal process of energy expenditure with the elimination of by-products through excretion. However, if this process does not take place regularly or efficiently, there will be an accumulation of fat molecules in the blood as well as in our body system.

With reference to the second and third sources, I might mention that there are certain culinary items that can augment accumulation of blood lipids by these two means. Alcohol is an example. Alcohol has been shown to increase lipids in both the tissues and the blood by enhancing endogenous synthesis of cholesterol and other lipids and by decreasing breakdown of these lipids from dietary intake (63). Interestingly, when alcohol mixed with garlic oil was fed to rats on a high fat diet, no increase of tissue or blood lipids was observed (63), indicating that garlic reduced endogenous lipogenesis and/or increased lipid breakdown. Having cited this study, let me hasten to add that I do not recommend that my patients drink happily away and hope garlic protects them. The long-term deleterious effect of alcohol on our body system is too high a price to pay by any standard.

Recent news of tragic deaths because of drug abuse has sobered many in America. Many in our country are hooked to drugs, both legal and illegal. Sadly, most people do not realize that the two major drugs ruining our society happen to be tobacco and alcohol, two very common and legal drugs! These two substances harm our lungs, liver, and other organs while affecting our physical and emotional health in a subtle but very sure way. If these two drugs could be controlled, many health problems would be avoided and fatal accidents relating to fire and drunk driving would be greatly reduced.

Getting back to the three main causes of high blood lipids, let's find out now how garlic affects them. The scientific data we have available demonstrate at least three possibilities 1) Garlic has been shown to either inhibit or reduce endogenous lipogenesis, 2) Garlic has been shown to increase breakdown of lipids and to enhance elimination of the breakdown by-products through the intestinal tract, and 3) Garlic has been shown to move the lipids from the tissue depot to the blood circulation and subsequently to be excreted from the body.

Several animal studies have demonstrated that components of garlic inhibit lipid synthesis by liver cells (27,28,31). Feeding rats garlic decreased the activity of several important enzymes involved in the synthesis of lipids not only in the liver but also in other adipose tissues such as fat pads (64,65,66). Incidentally, the study by Moses Adetumbi using yeast organisms (mentioned in Chapter 2) showed that garlic even prevented little yeast organisms from making lipids. So garlic is not only capable of keeping fat off of people, it can even keep microbes like yeast organisms slim, too!

Not long ago, a physician friend of mine after reading our paper (29), decided to put three of his patients with high risk for heart disease on garlic to reduce their blood lipids. These three gentlemen had several things in common: They had high cholesterol levels (over 300 mg/dl), each of them was about 50 pounds overweight, they were all truck drivers who smoked and drank a lot of beer, they all had a high fat diet consisting regularly of steak and ice cream, and they practically never exercised.

Anyway, while taking garlic supplement, their blood cholesterol continued to stay up. This doctor was not too concerned in the first three months since he knew from our study that a rise of cholesterol during the first three months of garlic feeding was to be expected. However, at six months their cholesterol levels continued to be high. We discussed the matter and speculated on several possibilities. One obvious possibility was that garlic simply was not working. Another possibility was that these gentlemen had such high fat levels in their body tissues that garlic was still moving them out from the tissue to the blood at six months. Thus, when we tested their blood, it continued to be high. Furthermore, because these subjects used alcohol frequently and heavily and had a high fat intake in their diets, they actually fulfilled all three requirements for having high blood lipids. We decided to investigate the second possibility.

Based on data from animal studies, we know that when there is a decrease of lipids in the organs such as the liver, there may be increased levels of lipids in the blood. So when these gentlemen continued to have high levels of lipids in the blood, my natural assumption was that there were less lipids in their livers. Obviously, this was only an assumption since we did not take a liver biopsy to prove it. At any rate, we decided to make some recommendations to these three men. We suggested that they cut down on rich desserts and heavy meals. They all objected to this since they felt their heavy work deserved heavy meals. We then suggested that they undertake a trial period of no alcohol for one month. Two of them consented. What was amazing was that at the end of one month, one gentleman's cholesterol level dropped from 320 mg/dl to 210 mg/dl, a drop of more than 100 mg/dl! In the other, the drop was from 340 to 280 mg/dl, also a very significant though less dramatic drop. These two cases proved our speculations and further show how much alcohol affects lipids.

One of these gentlemen, after experiencing this dramatic change in his blood chemistry decided on his own to completely give up alcohol and smoking. He also changed his diet and as a result has lost the extra pounds. In a recent check-up, this patient is in perfect health with a very much lower risk for coronary artery disease as predicted by the computer printout. The only thing the computer printout recommended was a regular exercise program. He would like to do this but finds himself too tired after a day's work to exercise. I suggested to him that every time he stops in a rest area he should run around for three to five minutes. I also recommended that he stop more often. Incidentally, this is the same recommendation I make to patients with varicose veins, lower back pain, and sciatica. By stopping every two hours to run for just a few minutes, their bodies and minds become refreshed. For those with varicose vein problems, wearing a light support hose during long trips is also most helpful.

Aside from cardiovascular disease, a very common medical problem my colleagues and I have been seeing in recent years is allergies. . . .

5

ALLERGIES, POLLUTION, AND TODAY'S LIFESTYLE

Alice and Betty are sisters from Singapore. They came to California for their college educations; Alice majored in science with plans to pursue a career in medicine, and Betty was a music major specializing in piano performance. Both did well during their first year—but during their second year in California, the problems began.

What problems? Both developed the symptoms of allergic rhinitis (hay fever)—runny nose, sneezing, and watery, itchy eyes. Physicians prescribed antihistamines; they relieved the symptoms to a degree, but packed with them a host of unpleasant side effects, including drowsiness, fatigue, dry mouth, and inability to concentrate. Skin tests indicated multiple allergies, but desensitization shots had little or no effect. It was back to antihistamines, switching from one brand to another in an attempt to reduce side effects. Nothing seemed to work. Alice's grades suffered; she received several C's and was understandably concerned about getting into medical school. Betty was no better: when she took her antihistamine, her concentration failed, her memory lapsed during performances, and she couldn't practice. If she failed to take the medication, her eyes and nose burned and itched. Finally their parents wrote to me for help: they had read a paper I had written about the use of acupuncture for allergic rhinitis (67); they had also heard rumors about an Oriental remedy of garlic for allergies. They asked for my recommendation, and I gave the girls their choice.

After one acupuncture treatment, both decided to try garlic (even the most "painless" acupuncture treatment involves some pain). I gave each a bottle of Kyolic garlic capsules and told each to take six a day.

That was several years ago. Within three weeks, each was free of hay fever symptoms. Alice finished medical school, and takes garlic capsules now only when the sky is blanketed with heavy smog. Betty graduated with a master's degree in music performance, and teaches in Singapore. Both are free of hay fever symptoms.

There's another interesting highlight to this story: Betty returns to California each year to visit Alice and other family members. After being free of hay fever symptoms all year in Singapore, she begins to sneeze as soon as she gets off the plane in Los Angeles. A few garlic capsules quickly control the problem—but it doesn't explain why Betty's allergy kicks up only on American soil.

Betty's not the only one. Many who come to the United States to live develop hay fever symptoms after a year or so. Most suffer with symptoms all year, with particular sensitivity to smoke fumes, automobile exhaust, smog, and air pollution.

The key could be chemicals and heavy metals found in our environment—especially in urban air. Fortunately, studies have shown that garlic can neutralize the toxic effect of various chemicals. We used our laboratory to test the detoxifying effect of garlic on heavy metals. Figure 7 shows ten test tubes each filled with 15 ml of a 5 percent suspension of human red blood cells. Tube 1 (C) contained 0.5 ml physiological saline and served as a control; Tube 2 (CK) had a 0.5 ml 1:10 dilution of Kyolic garlic extract in saline, and also served as a control. Other tubes—in pairs—contained heavy metals (lead, mercury, copper and aluminum) one in saline and the other in diluted Kyolic garlic extract. As is obvious in Figure 7,

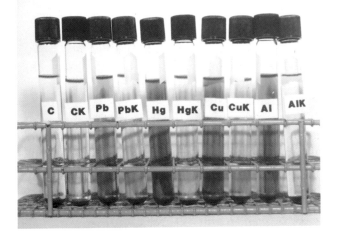

Figure 7. Prevention of lysis of red blood cells by garlic. C
and CK, controls with saline or Kyolic solution respec-
tively. Other tubes with metal ions showed lysis without
Kyolic and no lysis with Kyolic in tubes labeled with K. Pb
= lead, Hg = mercury, Cu = copper, Al = aluminum.

heavy metals caused the red blood cells to lyse. Even
small quantities of Kyolic prevented the lysis of red blood
cells.

Heavy metals are abundant both in nature and in urban
environments; lead, for example, is found in automobile
exhaust, paint, and batteries. Mercury, in addition to
being found in paint and batteries, contaminates sea fish
and has been used in dental fillings. If you have a healthy
immune system, you can usually cope with the toxic
effect of heavy metals; if not, you can become ill.

Many have researched the ability of garlic to aid in

detoxification. In one pilot study, Honolulu dentist Dr. Samuel Wong used garlic to treat fourteen patients with silver-mercury amalgam dental fillings. He found that garlic facilitated elimination of the mercury from the patients' systems, leading to detoxification (68).

Detoxification is normally accomplished by the liver— the largest organ in the human body. Besides regulating sugars and metabolizing lipids and proteins, the liver detoxifies alcohol, drugs, and other toxic chemicals that enter the body. When liver cells break down, the liver loses its function—and life is in jeopardy.

Since the liver is such an important organ, I would now like to share with you three recent studies by Japanese investigators showing garlic protecting against liver cell damage. In one study, researchers headed by Dr. Tohru Fuwa at the Central Research Laboratories of Wakunaga Pharmaceutical Company in Japan reported in the *Hiroshima Journal of Medical Sciences* (69) that four of the six sulfur-containing compounds isolated from garlic protected liver cells from damage caused by a toxic chemical carbon tetrachloride. The study was carried out in a rather sophisticated system in which liver cells were maintained in a tissue culture.

This finding was confirmed by Dr. Hiroshi Hikino and associates at the Pharmaceutical Institute of Tohoku University (70). They found that volatile oil and two sulfur-containing amino acids S-allylmercapto cysteine (ASSC) and S-methylmercapto cysteine (MSSC) extracted from garlic effectively prevented the damage of liver cells induced by carbon tetrachloride and D-galactosamine, two potent liver toxins. Interestingly, they also found that alliin, the precursor of the famous allicin, either did not protect against liver cell damage or did so poorly and certainly much less effectively than ASSC or MSSC, the two cysteine compounds. How do components of garlic protect liver damage? They further showed that garlic components exerted their protection by inhibiting the generation of free radicals and by preventing the oxidation of lipid peroxides and thus served as potent antioxidants.

The third study by Dr. Kyoichi Kagawa's group published in the *Japanese Journal of Pharmacology* looked into the therapeutic rather than the preventive value of garlic on liver damage (71). In Kagawa's study, garlic was given to mice by mouth six hours after they had been given carbon tetrachloride orally. Carbon tetrachloride damages liver cells by a process referred to as "fatty liver". When carbon tetrachloride (CCl_4) is introduced into liver tissue, it is converted to carbon trichloride (CCl_3) which then attacks unsaturated fatty acids in the liver to produce lipid peroxides resulting in the accumulation of triglycerides (fats) in the liver, thus "fatty liver". Dr. Kagawa's study showed that oral feeding of garlic extract even six hours after carbon tetrachloride poisoning was able to significantly inhibit the formation of fatty liver and thus protect the liver from injury induced by this toxic chemical. Incidentally, all these three papers were written in English so ardent students of garlic may want to read the original articles to get the information firsthand.

Besides pollution, we are concerned about the effects of radiation—so we conducted an experiment to determine whether garlic could provide protection against radiation. We incubated human lymphocytes in tissue cultures for two hours—both with and without Kyolic (2.5 mg/ml) or fresh garlic extract (also 2.5 mg/ml). We also set up tests using L-cysteine (1 mg/ml), a compound known to protect against radioactivity. We then irradiated all but one of each set of cultures with 2000 rads from a Therac-20 Linear Accelerator; each unradiated culture served as a control (UC).

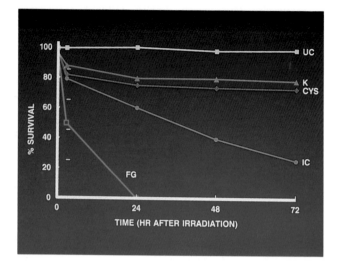

Figure 8. Protection of radiation damage. Unirradiated control (UC) remained viable throughout the experiment. Irradiation of 2000 rads (IC) resulted in death of 75% of lymphocytes at 72 hours. Fresh garlic (FG) caused death of 100% of cells in 24 hours. Protection of radiation damage was observed with Kyolic (K) and L-cysteine (CYS).

We tested viability of the cells with trypan blue dye three, twenty-four, forty-eight, and seventy-two hours following irradiation. The results are shown in Figure 8. The unirradiated lymphocytes (UC) remained viable in the tissue culture during the three-day period of observation. Irradiated control (IC) cultures not infused with protective agents steadily declined; within seventy-two hours, only 25 percent of the cells were still viable. Cells incubated with L-cysteine or Kyolic (CYS and K) enjoyed significant protection; a few cells died within the initial few minutes, but almost all others were viable at the end of the test period.

Interestingly, the fresh garlic extract (FG) proved extremely toxic to the lymphocytes. Many cells incubated with fresh garlic had died within three hours, and none survived beyond twenty-four hours.

The results of the cultures using fresh garlic raised a number of important questions. Our study showed that fresh garlic extract even in moderate dosage is toxic to lymphocytes. Other studies using fresh or raw garlic have demonstrated other unpleasant effects in addition to the strong odor. Large quantities of raw garlic may cause irritation of the digestive tract. Prolonged feeding of raw garlic to rats causes anemia, weight loss, and failure to grow (72). For this reason, individuals with existing digestive problems should use cooked garlic or choose a brand such as Kyolic which has removed irritating chemicals yet still retains its pharmacologic principles.

Another area of considerable interest to those of us involved in garlic research is its potential role in the prevention of cancer. . . .

6

GARLIC AND CANCER

Cancer is one of the most dreadful diseases of this modern age, ranking second only to heart disease as the most frequent cause of death in the United States. What causes cancer? There's no simple answer: many different factors probably lead to the development of cancer, with chemical carcinogens, radiation, and viruses among those known to us (73,74,75).

Some of the known causes still intrigue researchers, who struggle against time to find a cure. More than two hundred years ago, English surgeon Sir Percival Pott noted a high incidence of scrotal cancer among London's chimney sweeps (73). He correctly pinned fault on exposure to chimney soot—which we now know contains polycyclic hydrocarbons, known to cause cancer in animals. The chemicals in London's chimney soot is the same class of chemicals that filter into the lungs in cigarette smoke, increasing the risk of lung cancer. Scientists suspect that carcinogens result when some of these chemicals combine with foods and bacteria in the large intestine.

Another well-known cause of cancer is radiation (74), and much of what we know about radiation's effects comes from studies of people exposed to ionizing radiation. The list includes physicians and dentists who use X-rays for diagnosis or treatment; uranium miners; and nuclear industry personnel—as well as survivors of the nuclear bombings of Hiroshima and Nagasaki. Based on research, we believe that relatively high doses and long periods of exposure are necessary to produce cancer.

Still another cause of cancer—at least in animals—are

viruses (75). Researchers believe that viruses may also be involved in some human cancers, including hepatomas (liver cancers), some leukemias, lymphomas, and cancer of the cervix of the uterus. The herpes family of viruses— which cause canker sores, genital herpes, and infectious mononucleosis—is under the greatest suspicion.

For the past ten years, my associates and I have studied cancer biology and immunology (76,77,78,79,80). Ten years ago we reported that cancer cells secrete substances that repel cancer-fighting cells, particularly those we call phagocytes (76). As a result, our research has centered on ways to enhance phagocyte activity through various immune stimulants referred to as "biological response modifiers." We've experimented both with live bacterial vaccine and killed bacterial vaccine; both strengthen the body's control against cancer as long as three important conditions are met:

1. The tumor burden has to be low. In other words, the tumor has to be small—either because it has just begun to grow, or because most of it has been removed or destroyed by other means.

2. Dosage and the schedule of vaccine administration are important—and lower dosages generally work better than higher dosages. The concept "more is better" does not hold true to the use of these biological response modifiers.

3. The route of administration needs to provide optimal contact between the tumor cells and biological response modifier; local routes usually work better than systemic routes. (I'll discuss this in more detail later.)

We've also centered our research efforts on the role of nutrition in cancer development and prevention. An epidemiological study reported by the People's Republic of China several years ago (81) intrigued us. Researchers compared two large populations in the Shandong Province. Residents of the province's Cangshan County enjoyed the lowest death rate due to stomach cancer (3 per 100,000), but the county of Oixia residents had a thirteen-fold higher death rate due to the same cancer (40 per 100,000).

The difference?

The residents of Cangshan regularly eat 20 grams of garlic per day. The residents of Oixia rarely eat garlic. Why did garlic seem to make such a difference? The study showed that Cangshan residents had lower concentrations of nitrites in their gastric juices than those in Oixia who rarely eat garlic. In other words, garlic protected against the formation of nitrites - precursors of carcinogens - thus providing a protection against the development of stomach cancer.

Another group of Chinese researchers studied the effect of garlic and diallyl trisulfide (a component of garlic) on the growth of two human stomach cancers in the tissue cultures. They found that garlic and its component inhibited the growth of cancer cells as effectively as did some chemotherapeutic drugs (82).

What's the implication of these two studies?

The first study shows that garlic may well prevent carcinogen-induced cancer; the second shows that it may stop the growth of cancer cells. In other words, it may show promise for both prevention and treatment.

Many other studies bear out the same evidence. Studies conducted by Dr. Michael Wargovich in the Gastrointestinal Oncology Section at the Universitsy of Texas's M.D. Anderson Hospital showed that organic sulfides, including diallyl sulfide (an important component of garlic), inhibit the development of carcinogen dimethyl hydrazine-induced colon cancer (83,84). Studies by Dr. Sidney Belman at the New York University Medical Center involving mice showed that topical application of

garlic oil prevented skin cancer induced by dimethyl ben-
zanthracene (85). Researchers at the University of Minnesota at Minneapolis studied mice with benzopyrene-
induced stomach cancer. The administration of allyl
methyl trisulfide, a constituent of garlic oil, reduced 70
percent of the tumors during the period of the experiment (86). According to the Minnesota researchers, the
component in garlic stimulates an enzyme that protects
the stomach from the effects of the carcinogen.

During the past several years, I have collaborated with
several urologists in the study of bladder cancer (87,88,89);
as mentioned earlier, we have used both live and killed
bacterial vaccines and have included garlic extract in our
testing. Test results published in the *Journal of Urology*
(87,88) show that treatment with a liquid garlic extract
(Kyolic from Wakunaga Pharmaceutical) produced the
lowest incidence of bladder cancer (see Table 3). The
same treatment also resulted in smaller tumors (see Table
4).

What happens? Garlic apparently stimulates the body's
immune system, particularly enhancing the macrophages and lymphocytes, which destroy cancer cells (see
Figure 9).

Our best results occurred when garlic was applied
directly to the tumor site (see Figures 10 and 11). Figure 10
shows what happened when animals received only one
treatment one day after the tumor was transplanted. Control animals that received only saline had a progressive
increase in tumor size. When live vaccine (bacillus
Calmette-Guerin, abbreviated as BCG) was given systemically, the tumor was not reduced, but it was reduced
when the live vaccine was injected locally. The tumor
sizes were reduced when either garlic (*Allium sativum*,
abbreviated as AS) or the killed vaccine (*Corynebacterium parvum*, abbreviated as CP) was injected systemat-

ically—and even greater reduction occurred when the injection was local.

Table 3. Effect of intravesical immunotherapy on the incidence of bladder tumors—From (88) with permission.

Immune Stimulant Group	Treatment Schedule								
	Day 1			Day 6			Days 1 & 6		
	Tumor * Incidence	% With Tumors	P- ** Value	Tumor Incidence	% With Tumors	P- Value	Tumor Incidence	% With Tumors	P- Value
Control	14/20	70		12/17	71		15/21	71	
BCG	8/16	50	N.S.	12/20	60	N.S.	5/16	31	<0.02
CP	7/18	39	<0.01	10/16	63	N.S.	5/20	25	<0.005
AS	6/19	32	<0.02	7/18	39	0.01	5/21	24	<0.002
KLH	10/20	50	N.S.	9/19	47	N.S.	5/17	41	N.S.

* Number of mice with tumor/total number of mice in the group.
**Probability for t-test of means, compared with controls treated with saline. N.S. denotes not significant.

Table 4. Mean weights (in mg) of bladders and spleens per treatment group—From (88) with permission.

Immune Stimulant Group	Treatment Schedule					
	Day 1		Day 6		Days 1 & 6	
	Bladder	Spleen	Bladder	Spleen	Bladder	Spleen
Control (saline)	186 ± 14*	86 ± 7	174 ± 21	82 ± 7	231 ± 28	76 ± 9
BCG	130 ± 16	167 ± 11**	245 ± 36	212 ± 29**	144 ± 16	110 ± 8*
CP	70 ± 7**	178 ± 14**	136 ± 17	132 ± 17**	86 ± 8**	92 ± 7
AS	76 ± 6**	127 ± 13**	74 ± 6**	171 ± 14**	57 ± 7**	103 ± 6*
KLH	96 ± 11	76 ± 6	93 ± 7	66 ± 7	116 ± 11	71 ± 7

* Mean ± standard error.
** P value<0.05, compared with control on same treatment schedule.

Figure 11 shows what happened when similar tests were done involving five treatments. As illustrated in the figure, garlic (AS) and the killed vaccine (CP) showed much more positive results than did the live vaccine (BCG), which is currently used in the treatment of bladder cancer.

The most remarkable thing about this series of five treatments occurred when we examined the tumors under the microscope: what we had originally thought to

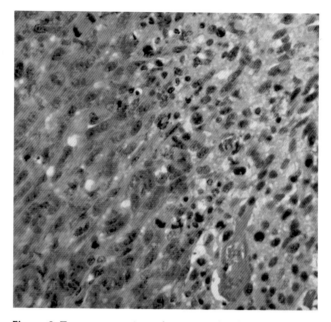

Figure 9. Tumor necrosis and margin of viable tumor with small lymphocytes and macrophages. Histiocytes have apparently cleared the nuclear debris, X310. From (87) with permission.

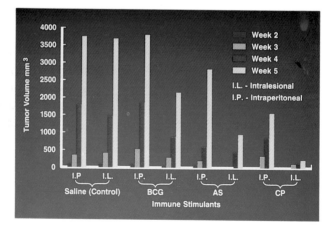

Figure 10. Comparison of IP versus IL immunotherapy one day after tumor transplant. From (87) with permission.

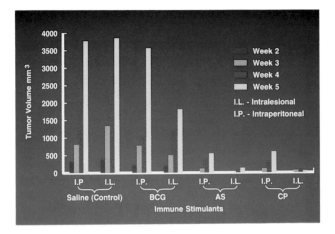

Figure 11. Comparison of IP versus IL immunotherapy - mice receiving five treatments on days 1, 3, 5, 7, and 9 after tumor transplant. From (87) with permission.

be smaller tumors treated by garlic or killed vaccine were actually only scar tissue. There were no tumor cells. In other words, five treatments with these agents actually cured the cancer! Note that the cure was obtained only with local injection, not systemic injection.

Nearly thirty years ago, researchers at Western Reserve University reported that garlic extract prevented tumor growth by inactivating sulfhydryl compounds of tumor cells (90,91). Our own studies show that garlic works in possibly a dual role, interfering with tumor cell metabolism on the one hand and stimulating immune cells on the other. Other investigators have also studied the immune modulating effects of garlic (92,93,94), which will be discussed in greater detail in the next chapter.

Current scientific evidence from China and the United States shows that garlic can prevent carcinogen-induced cancers in both animals and humans. We are understandably excited to see that a natural substance can have such impact on cancer prevention! Several energetic physicians and researchers are now working with me, using modern analytic tools to fully explore the effects of each component of garlic. So far, our evidence shows that garlic can help inhibit tumor growth—but we also have experimental data showing that garlic can enhance the body's own immune system. . . .

⑦

GARLIC AND THE
IMMUNE SYSTEM

Our immune system is like the United States Department of Defense: when it works as it should, it protects. against foreign invaders and maintains national peace. The Department of Defense employs various branches— the Army, Navy, Air Force, and Marines, to name a few— that help it do its job. Likewise, our immune system employs at least five major branches—the B lymphocytes, the T lymphocytes, the phagocytes, the killer cells, and the natural killer cells (see Figure 12).

The B lymphocytes respond to various stimuli by producing antibodies, which help fight off many common infections. The other four types of immune cells directly attack foreign invaders, such as cancer cells, bacteria, viruses, or fungi. Some carry out their attack by secreting powerful chemicals called cytokines; examples are interferons and interleukins (There are several varieties of each of these substances).

Our paper published in the *Journal of Urology* (87) explained that lymphocytes and macrophages were attracted to the site where garlic was injected. Other researchers have noticed that garlic extract attracts immune cells, so we decided to do a clear-cut study to see exactly how this happened.

We used three groups of mice in the study. The first group of mice received 0.1 ml of a 1:2 dilution of Kyolic liquid garlic extract injected subcutaneously into the inguinal (groin) area. The second received 0.1 ml of the diluted Kyolic liquid garlic extract injected systemically into the

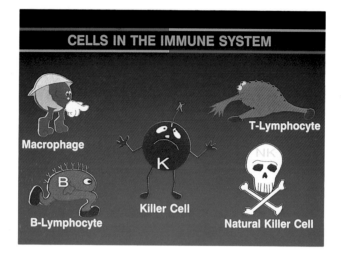

Figure 12. Five branches of military forces in host defense.

peritoneal cavity. The third group, which served as controls, did not receive any treatment.

Four days after we made the injections, we examined leukocytyes from the peritoneal cavity, spleens, and inguinal lymph nodes. Using sophisticated equipment - a computerized luminometer - we examined the cells to determine how well the leukocytes could engulf and destroy foreign particles; the results are shown in Figures 13A and 13B.

Figure 13A shows the leukocyte response of the mice that received injections of Kyolic into the groin. Compared to the control mice, those that received the local injections into the groin showed only slightly better leukocyte activity in the peritoneal cavity or spleen—but there was significantly greater leukocyte activity in the inguinal lymph nodes.

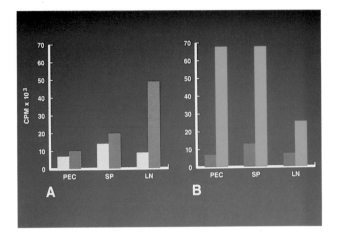

Figure 13. Enhancement of phagocytic activity was demonstrated using chemiluminescence assay. A. Mice were given Kyolic solution subcutaneously into the inguinal site. Compared with controls □, only slight increase of phagocytic activity was observed with leukocytes from the peritoneal cavity (PEC) and spleen (SP). Significantly higher activity was obtained with leukocytes from the inguinal lymph nodes (LN). B. Mice received Kyolic intraperitoneally. Compared with controls ■, increased activity was noted with all three sites; higher with cells from the peritoneal cavity (PEC) and spleen (SP).

Figure 13B shows the leukocyte response of the mice that received a systemic injection into the peritoneal cavity. Compared to the control mice, those that received systemic injections had significantly more leukocyte activity in the peritoneal cavity and spleen—clearly more than in the inguinal lymph nodes. Obviously, if the disease is localized, a localized treatment should be given, whereas systemic disease should be treated with a systemic treatment. In other words, systemic therapy shouldn't always be the automatic choice of treatment.

Similar findings have been confirmed in other studies. One study in Japan showed that certain fractions of Kyolic garlic extract stimulated macrophages to kill tumor cells and to clear carbon particles from animals' bodies. The same researchers showed that garlic fractions stimulate B lymphocytes, the type of cells that produce antibodies (95).

What about data on humans? Florida pathologist Dr. Tariq Abdullah and his associates tested volunteer subjects and reported their findings to the Federation of American Societies for Experimental Biology (96). Volunteers were divided randomly into three groups. The first took 0.5 gm/kg body weight of raw garlic every day for three weeks. The second group took 1800 mg of Kyolic (six capsules) every day for three weeks. The third group used no garlic and served as controls.

At the end of three weeks, researchers took blood samples from each volunteer and used the blood on tumor cells in a laboratory culture; they wanted to see how active each volunteer's natural killer cells were against the tumor cells. The natural killer cells of those who ate raw garlic killed 139 percent more tumor cells than the natural killer cells of those who did not eat garlic. The natural killer cells of those who took Kyolic capsules killed 159 percent more tumor cells than the natural killer cells of those who did not eat garlic. Incidentally, the Florida team believes that heat or cooking may destroy some of garlic's important constituents, so they chose Kyolic—the commercial garlic preparation that is not processed with heat.

Finally, many researchers believe that stress is a causative—or at least contributing—factor in the development of cancer. Could garlic possibly help the human body cope with the effects of stress? To find out, keep reading. . . .

STRESS—
THE HIDDEN CAUSE OF DISEASE

We are living in a world full of stress. Nearly all the patients who consult my office will, sooner or later, confide to me that they are under a lot of stress. I learned early in my practice that my willingness to listen to their problems was vital for their recovery from illness, and that unless the stress level is reduced, it is futile to expect full restoration of physical health. In other words, as long as a patient is under stress, he is in distress. There are many papers now documenting that stress impairs our immune system, making it difficult for us to fight infection and even cancer (97,98,99). Different people may be exposed to different kinds of stresses: environmental, physical, and psychosocial are some of the major ones. Environmental factors: noise, living condition, air, odor, extremes of temperature, can all bring stress to an individual. Other individuals may suffer stress because of certain physical discomforts or certain mechanical factors. Still others are victimized by psychosocial stress related to interpersonal relationships with family members, coworkers, and others. It is probably safe to say that every one of us, at one time or another, experiences stress at various degrees. Stress is not necessarily detrimental. A certain amount is necessary to motivate us to do our very best. So stress can actually be beneficial if managed effectively. Now what does garlic have to do with stress?

A certain Oriental tale tells of garlic's ability to help one cope with stress. Let's say that Mr. A is mad at Mr. B and finds Mr. B's mere presence stressful to him. Mr. A thus takes raw garlic and reports that Mr. B no longer gives him stress. Whether or not this is because the odor of raw garlic keeps the troublesome Mr. B away, I am not sure.

At any rate, I have in front of me three papers published by Dr. Tohru Fuwa and associates in Japan describing the effect of garlic on stress (100,101,102). In one study the researchers randomly divided mice into three groups. The first group was subjected to cold temperatures (environmental stress); the second group was put in a box that was mounted on an oscillator that shook the box at 129 cycles per minute for four hours (physical stress). The third group was subjected to rope climbing (also a physical stress). Researchers noted that the stresses caused the mice to behave abnormally; all suffered loss of motor coordination, extreme fatigue, and loss of appetite.

Half of the mice were then given garlic (Kyolic liquid extract), and the experiment was repeated. Those who ate the Kyolic were able to maintain motor coordination, recover rapidly from fatigue, and function more efficiently than those who did not eat garlic.

In another study, the researchers restrained a group of mice for twelve hours a day for four consecutive days—an experiment designed to mimic the effects of psychosocial stress. At the end of the four days, the mice showed markedly reduced weight of the spleen and thymus and markedly fewer B lymphocytes with which to fight infection. In other words, researchers found that stress can impair the function of the immune system. When part of the mice were supplemented with garlic extract, no weight loss occurred and the optimum number of B lymphocytes was restored, boosting the immune system.

One of the main symptoms of stress, regardless of its source, is lack of energy; the victim of stress tires easily, becomes depressed, lacks motivation, and is filled with dread. In animal studies, stress causes a loss of strength and reduces endurance. A group of Indian investigators tested the effects of garlic on stress-crippled physical endurance to determine whether garlic could boost endurance (103). Endurance for the study was measured by how long rats were able to keep swimming.

For the study, different groups of rats were given varying dosages of garlic juice or oil for a period of seven days; the control rats were given saline. Researchers then measured how long the rats could keep swimming before becoming too fatigued to continue. The rats were then injected with isoproterenol, a drug that damages the heart muscle, and swimming endurance was again measured.

The control rats—those who received only saline—swam for an average of 480 seconds before the isoproterenol injection, and only 78 seconds after the injection. But the rats that had been fed garlic for seven

Table 5. Effect of pretreatment with garlic on physical endurance in rats challenged with isoproterenol (IP).

Group fed*	Swimming time (seconds)		Percent Diminution
	Before IP	After IP	
Saline	480	78	84
Garlic Juice 1 ml/day × 7	516	352	32
Garlic oil 1 mg/day × 7	840	560	33

* Ten rats in each group. Adapted from (103) with permission.

days swam for an average of 840 seconds before and 560 seconds after the isoproterenol injection (see Table 5). This study proved two things: garlic boosted normal endurance (the rats fed garlic swam longer to begin with), and garlic also helped protect the rats even after their

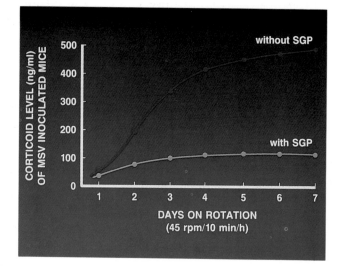

Figure 14. Effect of SGP on "stress horomone". Animals
subjected to hourly rotation as a form of physical stress
(red circle) had steady increased levels of corticoid,
whereas feeding with SGP significantly minimized this
increase.

heart muscles had been damaged by isoproterenol.

As we have repeated this experiment for students in
our own laboratory, with the same results, I am reminded
that Egyptian pharaohs prescribed extra rations of garlic
to builders working on the massive pyramids to help
enhance strength and endurance.

In an effort to measure garlic's effects on stress, my
associates and I tested mice with Moloney sarcoma virus
(MSV) induced tumors. Simply stated, we used a "stress
machine" to test the mice that had MSV tumors. Our
stress machine, developed by a Seattle-based microbiol-
ogist, was a modified phonograph that had the capacity
to turn at various speeds.

We placed the mice on top of the machine and rotated it at 45 rpms for ten minutes every hour. One group of mice was fed a regular laboratory diet. The second group was fed the same diet supplemented with 25 mg per day per mouse of a special garlic preparation (SGP powder from Wakunaga Pharmaceutical).

At the end of a week, we measured the levels of blood corticoid—the "stress hormone" that is secreted by the body when an animal or human is under stress. The mice on a regular diet had blood corticoid levels of 500 ng/ml; those who took garlic supplements had dramatically lower levels of 100 ng/ml—only one-fifth the stress hormone (see Figure 14). After the third week, we measured tumor volume in the two groups of mice. Those on a regular diet showed a progressive increase in the size of

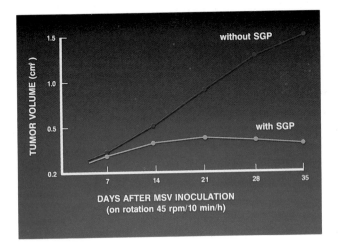

Figure 15. The increase in coricoid in Fig. 14 is correlated with progressive increase in tumor volume. Animals supplemented with SGP had slow and minimal rise of tumor volume. Is it because they could cope better with stress?

tumors; those who ate garlic had growth of tumors until the third week, after which there was a slow but steady reduction in the size of tumors (see Figure 15).

I would now like to share with you three clinical studies conducted by Japanese investigators showing the impact of garlic on stress. In the first, more than a thousand patients in seven university-teaching hospitals including those at Hiroshima and Tokyo Universities were tested to determine whether garlic extract affected psychosomatic complaints. Each patient was given 2 ml of Kyolic every day for four weeks. At the end of the four-week test period, 50 to 80 percent of the patients who ate Kyolic suffered less fatigue, depression, and anxiety (104).

Another study involved patients with gynecological malignancies who underwent radiotherapy and/or chemotherapy. Those patients who took two capsules of Kyolic a day for 30 to 270 days enjoyed significantly fewer side effects from the radiotherapy and chemotherapy. In fact, 67 percent of the women who took Kyolic reported having absolutely no side effects while they were taking their regular therapy (105).

Still another study by medical researchers at Sakitama Hospital involved two groups of hospitalized patients. The first group of twenty patients took four capsules of Kyolic a day for fifty days; the control group took a placebo for the same period (106). At the end of the test period, the Kyolic group showed more rapid recovery from exhaustion, had fewer complaints of fatigue after manual labor, and reported less feeling of cold in the extremities than did the placebo group. Interestingly, those over fifty years of age benefited more from the Kyolic in terms of endurance, possibly because younger patients had a higher reserve of energy.

In my own work with stressed patients, I have noted that those who use garlic regularly suffer much less from

the effects of stress. Without rigid scientific experimenta-
tion to measure the differences, I can't make a medical
statement as to why. The effect may be a placebo—but, if
so, it's certainly a powerful one! If you're interested in the
power of a placebo, read the remarkable experience of
Norman Cousins in *Anatomy of an Illness* (107).

CONCLUSION
THE TRIANGLE OF DISEASE

Dear Reader, I have enjoyed communicating with you through these pages, and I hope you have enjoyed reading them. In concluding this book, I would like to share with you a concept that I have used in my teaching for a number of years. So please sit back, relax, and pretend

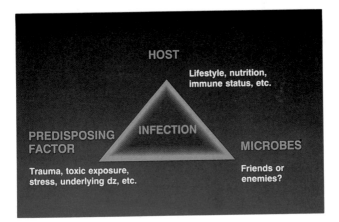

Figure 16. The triangle of infection is used to illustrate the three aspects of a disease process.

you are in an auditorium with 150 or more of my students. The class has just begun. My energetic students have their eyes wide open wondering what knowledge their teacher has to convey to them today. The concept is called "The Triangle of Disease." I usually will flash on the screen a slide showing the triangle which you can now see on Figure 16.

The disease process can be illustrated using a triangle: the three angles are: the etiology (Webster defines it as "the assignment of a cause or reason"), the susceptible host, and predisposing factors. If we use infection as an example, the three angles are 1) microbes as the etiologic agent, 2) a susceptible host or a person who is susceptible because of impaired immunity, impaired phagocytic function, poor nutrition and/or a risky lifestyle determining the susceptibility, and 3) certain factors such as trauma, toxic exposure, stress and underlying disease which predispose a person to infection.

Looking at the triangle, one needs to recognize that microorganisms alone do not usually cause infection unless there is a susceptible host, even though we give the textbook definition of infection as an invasion of the body by microorganisms. The concept that I want to put across to you is that microorganisms alone do not usually cause infection unless there is a susceptible human being or animal. Having said that, let me hasten to add that even with a susceptible host and the presence of microbes, there may still not be an infection unless the process is triggered by certain predisposing factors. For this reason, in the prevention or treatment of an infectious disease, we need to look at all three angles rather than just one of these angles. Merely killing the microbes may not be the best solution. Indeed often carried with it is the price of unwanted side effects. Typical examples are yeast infections such as Candida oral thrush and Candida vaginitis following the use of a broad spectrum antibiotic.

In the case of infection we obviously need to consider microbes as the primary factor with host and predisposing factors as secondary factors. However, it is equally important to bear in mind when considering a disease that all three angles have equal weight or significance. An example of a clinical entity I often use with my medical students is diarrhea. Someone has estimated that in the world each day there are 20 million people suffering from diarrhea. We all know that often our diarrhea is simply due to eating the wrong kind of food. In other words, it may not have anything to do with the microbes. In the figure under microbes, I have "friends or enemies." The point I want to make is it may not be easy to know which microbe is the enemy and which is the friend. Let's say a person eats the wrong kind of food and has diarrhea. If he consults a physician and gets a course of antibiotic, he will then be killing the friendly bacteria without touching the enemy at all, since there isn't any enemy to begin with. Looking at the third angle, the predisposing factors, it is my practice to constantly remind my students that this angle is a very important one. It too may be the primary cause of a complaint, rather than secondary. Again, take the complaint of diarrhea. It is true that we do not want to miss those germs like *Salmonella*, *Shigella*, *Campylobacter*, and *Vibrio* that are famous intestinal pathogens. What I want to remind them is that before they write a prescription for a potent drug, find out and *study* what drugs the patient has been taking. In my own experience, I have seen case after case of a patient complaining of diarrhea or another gastrointestinal discomfort due to one or more drugs received from a doctor. An assignment I have given my students is to check the *Physicians' Desk Reference* (PDR) to make a list of drugs without gastrointestinal side effects. The current PDR has more than

2000 pages. The lesson to be learned from this exercise is that there are very few drugs in the big book without gastrointestinal side effects! So let me make a short conclusive remark regarding the triangle: each of the three angles can have equal importance.

It is important to point out that this triangle and its basic principle applies not only to infection but also to most, if not all, major diseases inflicting the human race. For example, we can change the entity from infection to cancer and all we need to modify is just one of the triangles - adding chemical carcinogens and radiation to the microbes. We mentioned previously the three well-known causes (etiology) of cancer: carcinogens, radiation, and viruses. With that in mind, the prevention and treatment of cancer should thus encompass all three angles. Merely killing the viruses is not the solution. For that matter, current methods of aiming only at killing cancer cells is not adequate. One needs to strengthen the host and to remove the predisposing factor in order to obtain a satisfactory and lasting result.

What about AIDS? The same principle applies here. Methods aimed at killing viruses are not useful. Whatever kills viruses most likely will also harm the cells which support the growth of the viruses. One needs to strengthen the host through lifestyle modification and proper nutrition. Oh, yes, predisposing factors which are the most important, need to be removed. Drugs and toxic materials that suppress the immune system can no longer be tolerated.

Can garlic be used to treat AIDS? That's a very difficult question; once the disease is fully developed, it is not likely that any single agent or approach will be effective in its treatment. That brings us to a second critical question: could garlic possibly help prevent AIDS?

I think it can.

Why? Because, as I look at the triangle of disease, I recall all I have learned about garlic: garlic can inhibit the growth of viruses, garlic enhances the function of phago-cytes and natural killer cells, and garlic nullifies some of the toxins that impair the immune system.

It thus appears that this natural product has all the good qualities to ensure a healthy host. For this reason, I believe it can be used to advantage together with a sound, healthful lifestyle to prevent a disease even as dreadful as AIDS.

Quite a few years ago, I came across a book entitled *The Ministry of Healing* written by Ellen G. White almost a century ago (108). I was impressed with a statement on page 127 of this book where she says, "In case of sickness, the cause should be ascertained. Unhealthful conditions should be changed, wrong habits corrected. Then nature is to be assisted in her effort to expel impurities and to re-establish right conditions in the system." Let's apply this statement to our triangle: In case of sickness (again, let's say in this case we are dealing with infection), we are to do five things:

1. Cause should be ascertained (not just the microbes but the whole triangle).
2. Unhealthful conditions should be changed (this means maybe we need to change our lifestyle).
3. Wrong habits should be corrected (how about dietary habits).
4. Assist nature to expel impurities (toxic exposure maybe).
5. Re-establish right conditions in the system.

Maybe at this moment the question you have in your mind is "What does garlic have to do with this?" Please read point number four again. Garlic can help our bodies expel impurities. We have discussed in previous chapters that garlic detoxifies the system of heavy metal poisoning, protects against irradiation, and even kills microbes.

Looking at the triangle again, we will see that components of garlic actually encompass all three angles. It is amazing that nature has provided us with such an "all around" product that is useful for one's health. Have you had your garlic today? When I ask this question, what I am really asking is: Have you done something today to keep the triangle balanced? If your answer is "not yet" or "not quite", it is time then to adjust your thinking and to begin a regular program that will enhance your health and well being. If your answer is "yes", you're then on your way to enjoying life's fullness! As you proceed on that wonderful journey, make sure you share your health secrets with friends and loved ones—and together you'll discover nature's key to good health!

BIBLIOGRAPHY

1. Fenwick GR, Hanley AB: The genus *Allium* - Part 1. CRC Crit Rev Food Sci Nutr 22:199, 1985.
2. Fenwick GR, Hanley AB: The genus *Allium* - Part 2. CRC Crit Rev Food Sci Nutr 22:273, 1985.
3. Fenwick GR, Hanley AB: The genus *Allium* - Part 3. CRC Crit Rev Food Sci Nutr 23:1, 1985.
4. Hanley AB, Fenwick GR: Cultivated Alliums. J Plant Foods 6:211, 1985.
5. Block E: The chemistry of garlic and onions. Sci Am 252:114, 1985.
6. Fliermans CB: Inhibition of *Histoplasma capsulatum* by garlic. Mycopathol Mycol Appl 50:227, 1973.
7. Tansey MR, Appleton JA: Inhibition of fungal growth by garlic extract. Mycologia 67:409, 1975.
8. Appleton JA, Tansey MR: Inhibition of growth of zoopathogenic fungi by garlic extract. Mycologia 67:882, 1975.
9. Barone FE, Tansey MR: Isolation, purification, identification, synthesis, and kinetics of activity of the anticandidal components of *Allium sativum* and a hypothesis for its mode of action. Mycologia 69:793, 1977.
10. Fromtling R, Bulmer GS: In vitro effect of aqueous extract of garlic (*Allium sativum*) on the growth and viability of *Cryptococcus neoformans*. Mycologia 70:397, 1978.
11. Delaha EC, Garagusi VF: Inhibition of mycobacteria by garlic extract (*Allium sativum*). Antimicrob Agents Chemother 27:485, 1985.
12. Adetumbi MA, Lau BHS: Inhibition of in vitro germination and spherulation of *Coccidioides immitis* by *Allium sativum*. Current Microbiol 13:73, 1986.
13. Adetumbi MA, Javor GT, Lau BHS: *Allium sativum*

(garlic) inhibits lipid synthesis by *Candida albicans*. Antimicrob Agents Chemother 30:499, 1986.

14. Adetumbi MA, Lau BHS: *Allium sativum* (garlic) - a natural antibiotic. Med Hypotheses 12:227, 1983.

15. Prasad G, Sharma VD: Efficacy of garlic (*Allium sativum*) treatment against experimental candidiasis in chicks. Brit Vet J 136:448, 1980.

16. Amer M, Taha M, Tosson Z: The effect of aqueous garlic extract on the growth of dermatophytes. Int J Dermatol 19:285, 1980.

17. Hunan Medical College, China. Garlic in cryptococcal meningitis. A preliminary report of 21 cases. Chinese Med J 93:123, 1980.

18. Tjia TL, Yeow YK, Tan CB: Cryptococcal meningitis. J Neurol Neurosurg Psych 48:853, 1985.

19. Tutakne MA, Bhardwaj JR, Satyanarayanan G, Sethi IC: Sporotrichosis treated with garlic juice. Indian J Dermatol 28:40, 1983.

20. Tsai Y, Cole LL, Davis LE, Lockwood SJ, Simmons V, Wild GC: Antiviral properties of garlic: In vitro effects on influenza B, herpes simplex and coxsackie viruses. Planta Medica 5:460, 1985.

21. Nagai K: Experimental studies on the preventive effect of garlic extract against infection with influenza virus. Japanese J Inf Dis 47:321, 1973.

22. Esanu V, Prahoveanu E: The effect of garlic extract, applied as such or in association with NaF, on experimental influenza in mice. Rev Roum Med Virol 34:11, 1983.

23. Chaudhury DS, Sreenivasamurthy V, Jayaraj P, Sreekantiah KR, Johar DS: Therapeutic usefulness of garlic in leprosy. J Indian Med Assoc 39:517, 1962.

24. Varon S: Medical student discovers curative powers of garlic. Heritage p. 28, April 10, 1987.

25. Block E, Ahmad S, Mahendra JK, Crecely RW, Apitz-

Castro R, Cruz, MR: Ajoene: a potent antithrombotic agent from garlic. J Am Chem Soc 106:8295, 1984.

26. Yoshida S, Kasuga S, Hayashi N, Ushiroguchi T, Matsuura H, Nakagawa S: Antifungal activity of ajoene derived from garlic. Appl Environ Microbiol 53:615, 1987.

27. Qureshi AA, Din ZZ, Abuirmeileh N, Burger WC, Ahmad Y, Elson CE: Suppresion of avian hepatic lipid metabolism by solvent extracts of garlic: impact on serum lipids. J Nutr 113:1746, 1983.

28. Qureshi AA, Abuirmeileh N, Din ZZ, Elson CE, Burger WC: Inhibition of cholesterol and fatty acid biosynthesis in liver enzymes and chicken hepatocytes by polar fractions of garlic. Lipids 18:343, 1983.

29. Lau BHS, Lam F, Wang-Cheng R: Effect of an odor-modified garlic preparation on blood lipids. Nutr Res 7:139, 1987.

30. Bordia A: Effect of garlic on blood lipids in patients with coronary heart disease. Am J Clin Nutr 34:2100, 1981.

31. Chang ML, Johnson MA: Effect of garlic on carbohydrate metabolism and lipid synthesis in rats. J Nutr 110:931, 1980.

32. Chi MS, Koh ET, Stewart TJ: Effects of garlic on lipid metabolism in rats fed cholesterol or lard. J Nutr 112:241, 1982.

33. Jain RC: Onion and garlic in experimental cholesterol atherosclerosis in rabbits. I. Effect of serum lipids and development of atherosclerosis. Artery 1:115, 1975.

34. Nakamura H, Ishikawa M: Effect of S-methyl-1-cysteine sulfoxide on cholesterol metabolism. Kanzo 12:673, 1971.

35. Kritchevsky D, Tepper SA, Morrisey R, Klurfeld D: Influence of garlic oil on cholesterol metabolism in

rats. Nutr Reports Int 22:641, 1980.

36. Lau BHS, Adetumbi MA, Sanchez A: *Allium sativum* (garlic) and atherosclerosis: a review. Nutr Res 3:119, 1983.

37. Miller GJ, Miller NE: Plasma-high-density-lipoprotein concentration and development of ischaemic heart-disease. Lancet 1:16, 1975.

38. Carew TE, Hayes SB, Koschinsky T, Steinberg D: A mechanism by which high-density lipoproteins may slow the atherogenic process. Lancet 1:1315, 1976.

39. Sassa H, Ito JT, Niwa T, Matsui E: Fibrinolysis in patients with ischemic heart disease. Japanese Circulat J 39:525, 1975.

40. Chakrabarti R, Hocking ED, Fearnley GR: Fibrinolytic activity and CAD. Lancet 1:987, 1968.

41. Lau BHS: Anticoagulant and lipid regulating effects of garlic (*Allium sativum*). In *New Protective Roles of Selected Nutrients in Human Nutrition*, Gene A. Spiller and James Scala, editors, Alan R. Liss, publisher, 1988.

42. Sainani GS, Desai DB, Gorhe NH, Natu SM, Pise DV, Sainani PG: Dietary garlic, onion and some coagulation parameters in Jain community. J Asso Phys India 27:707, 1979.

43. Sainani GS, Desai DB, Gorhe NH, Natu SM, Pise DV, Sainani PG: Effect of dietary garlic and onion on serum lipid profile in Jain community. Indian J Med Res 69:776, 1979.

44. Sainani GS, Desai DB, More KN: Onion, garlic and atherosclerosis. Lancet 1:575, 1976.

45. Bolton S, Null G, Troetel WM: The medical uses of garlic - fact and fiction. Am Pharm 22:448, 1985.

46. Loeper M, Debray M: Antihypertensive action of garlic extract. Bull Soc Med 37:1032, 1921.

47. Piotrowski G: L'ail en therapeutique. Praxis 488, 1948.

48. Papayannopoulos G: Garlic. Lancet 2:962, 1969.
49. Srinivasan V: A new antihypertensive agent. Lancet 2:800, 1969.
50. Zheziang Institute of Traditional Chinese Medicine: The effect of essential oil of garlic on hyperlipemia and platelet aggregation. J Trad Chinese Med 6:117, 1986.
51. Bordia A, Bansal HC: Essential oil of garlic in prevention of atherosclerosis. Lancet 2:1491, 1973.
52. Petkov V: A pharmacological study of garlic (*Allium sativum* L.). Annuaire de l'Universite de Sofia, Faculte de Medecine, t. XXVIII 885, 1949.
53. Petkov V: On the action of garlic (*Allium sativum* L.) on the blood pressure. Sovremenna Medizina 1:5, 1950.
54. Petkov V: New experimental data about the pharmacodynamics of some plant species. Sofia: Nauka i Iskustve 227, 1953.
55. Petkov V: Uber die Pharmakodynamik einiger in Bulgarien wildwashsender bzw angebauter Arzneipflanzen. Zeitschreift fur arztliche Fortbildung 56:430, 1962.
56. Petkov V, Stoev V, Bakalov D, Petev L: The Bulgarian drug Satal as a remedy for lead intoxication in industrial conditions. Higiena Truda i Profesionalnie Zabolevania 4:42, 1965.
57. Petkov V: Plants with hypotensive, antiatheromatous and coronarodilatating action. Am J Chinese Med 3:197, 1979.
58. Mancia G, Grassi G, Pomidossi G, Gregorini L, Bertinieri G, Parati G, Ferrari A, Zancchetti A: Effects of blood-pressure measurement by the doctor on patient's blood pressure and heart rate. Lancet 2:695, 1983.
59. Jain RC, Vyas CR, Mahatma OP: Hypoglycaemic

action of onion and garlic. Lancet 2:1491, 1973.

60. Bordia A, Bansal HC: Essential oil of garlic in prevention of atherosclerosis. Lancet 2:1491, 1973.

61. Jain RC, Vyas CR: Garlic in alloxan-induced diabetic rabbits. Am J Clin Nutr 28:684, 1975.

62. Nagai K, Nakagawa S, Nojima S, Mimori H: Effect of aged garlic extract on glucose tolerance test in rats. Basic Pharmacol Therapeut 3:45, 1975.

63. Shoetan A, Augusti KT, Joseph PK: Hypolipidemic effects of garlic oil in rats fed ethanol and a high lipid diet. Experientia 40:261, 1984.

64. Itokawa Y, Inoue K, Sasagawa S, Fujiwara M: Effect of S-methylcysteine and related sulfur-containing amino acids on lipid metabolism of experimental hypercholesterolemic rats. J Nutr 103:88, 1973.

65. Chi MS: Effects of garlic products on lipid metabolism in cholesterol-fed rats. Proc Soc Exp Bio Med 171:174, 1982.

66. Adoga GI, Osuoi J: Effect of garlic oil extract on serum, liver and kidney enzymes of rats fed on high sucrose and alcohol diets. Biochem Int 13:615, 1986.

67. Lau BHS, Wong DS, Slater JM: Effect of acupuncture on allergic rhinitis: clinical and laboratory evaluations. Am J Chinese Med 3:236, 1975.

68. Wong SJ, Zhu DA: The effectiveness of S.G.P. on dental patients with mercury restorations - a pilot study. Personal Communication, 1987.

69. Nakagawa S, Yoshida S, Hirao Y, Kasuga S, Fuwa T: Cytoprotective activity of components of garlic, ginseng and ciuwjia on hepatocyte injury induced by carbon tetrachloride in vitro. Hiroshima J Med Sci 34:303, 1985.

70. Hikino H, Tohkin M, Kiso Y, Namiki T, Nishimura S, Takeyama K: Antihepatotoxic actions of *Allium sativum* bulbs. Planta Medica 3:163, 1986.

71. Kagawa K, Matsutaka H, Yamaguchi Y, Fukuhama C: Garlic extract inhibits the enhanced peroxidation and production of lipids in carbon tetrachloride-induced liver injury. Japanese J Pharmacol 42:19, 1986.

72. Nakagawa S, Masamoto K, Sumiyoshi H, Kunihiro K, Fuwa T: Effect of raw and extracted-aged garlic juice on growth of young rats and their organs after peroral administration. J Toxicol Sci 5:91,1980.

73. Wigley C: Chemical carcinogenesis and precancer. In *Introduction to the Cellular and Molecular Biology of Cancer*. L.M. Franks and N. Teich, editors. p. 131, 1986.

74. Adams GE: Radiation carcinogenesis. In *Introduction to the Cellular and Molecular Biology of Cancer*. L.M. Franks and N. Teich, editors. p. 154, 1986.

75. Wyke, JA: Viruses and cancer. In *Introduction to the Cellular and Molecular Biology of Cancer*. L.M. Franks and N. Teich, editors. p. 176, 1986.

76. Lau BHS, Masek TD, Chu WT, Slater JM: Antiinflammatory reaction associated with murine L1210 leukemia. Experientia 32:1598, 1976.

77. Slater JM, Ngo E, Lau BHS: Effect of therapeutic irradiation on the immune responses. Am J Roentg 26:313, 1976.

78. Johnson JA, Lau BHS, Nutter RL, Slater JM, Winter CE: Effect of L1210 leukemia on the susceptibility of mice to *Candida albicans* infections. Infect Immun 19:146, 1978.

79. Tosk J, Lau BHS, Myers RC, Torrey R: Selenium-induced enhancement of hematoporphyrin derivative phototoxicity in murine bladder tumor cells. Biochem Biophys Res Comm 104:1086, 1986.

80. Lau BHS, Wang-Cheng RM, Tosk J: Tumor-specific T-lymphocyte cytoxicity enhanced by low dose of C.

parvum. J Leukocyte Biol 41:407, 1987.

81. Mei X, Wang ML, Xu HX, Pan XP, Gao CY, Han N, Fu MY: Garlic and gastric cancer. Acta Nutr Sinica 4:53, 1982.

82. Pan XY: Comparison of the cytotoxic effect of fresh garlic, diallyl trisulfide, 5-fluorouracil, mitomycin C and cis-DDP on two lines of gastric cancer cells. Chung-Hua Chung Liu Tsa Chih 7:103, 1985.

83. Wargovich MJ, Goldberg MT: Diallyl sulfide: a naturally occurring thioether that inhibits carcinogen-induced nuclear damage to colon epithelial cells in vivo. Mutation Res 143:127, 1985.

84. Wargovich MJ: Diallyl sulfide, a flavor component of garlic (*Allium sativum*), inhibits dimethylhydrazine-induced colon cancer. Carcinogenesis 8:487, 1987.

85. Belman S: Onion and garlic oils inhibit tumor promotion. Carcinogenesis 4:1063, 1983.

86. Sparnins VL, Mott AW, Barany G, Wattenberg LW: Effects of allyl methyl trisulfide on glutathione S-transferase activity and benzopyrene-induced neoplasia in the mouse. Nutr Cancer 8:211, 1986.

87. Lau BHS, Woolley JL, Marsh CL, Barker GR, Koobs DH, Torrey RR: Superiority of intralesional immunotherapy with *Corynebacterium parvum* and *Allium sativum* in control of murine transitional cell carcinoma. J Urol 136:701, 1986.

88. Marsh CL, Torrey RR, Woolley JL, Barker GR, Lau BHS: Superiority of intravesical immunotherapy with *Corynebacterium parvum* and *Allium sativum* in control of murine bladder cancer. J Urol 137:359, 1987.

89. Lau BHS, Marsh CL, Barker GR, Woolley J, Torrey R: Effects of biological response modifiers on murine bladder tumor. Nat Immun Cell Growth Regul 4:260, 1985.

90. Weisberger AS, Pensky J: Tumor-inhibiting effects

derived from an active principle of garlic (*Allium sativum*). Science 126:1112, 1957.

91. Weisberger AS, Pensky J: Tumor inhibition by a sulfhydryl-blocking agent related to an active principle of garlic (*Allium sativum*). Cancer Res 18:1301, 1958.

92. Fujiwara M, Nakata T: Induction of tumour immunity with tumour cells treated with extract of garlic (*Allium sativum*). Nature 216:83, 1967.

93. Nakata T, Fujiwara M: Adjuvant action of garlic sugar solution in animals immunized with ehrlich ascites tumor cells attenuated with allicin. Gann 66:417, 1975.

94. Aboul-Enein AM: Inhibition of tumor growth with possible immunity by Egyptian garlic extracts. Die Nahrung 30:161, 1986.

95. Hirao Y, Sumioka I, Nakagami S, Yamamoto M, Hatono S, Yoshida S, Fuwa T, Nakagawa S: Activation of immunoresponder cells by the protein fraction from aged garlic extract. Phytotherapy Res, 1:161, 1987.

96. Kandil OM, Abdullah TH, Elkadi A: Garlic and the immune system in humans: its effect on natural killer cells. Federation Proceedings 46:441, 1987.

97. Ader R: Psychoneuroimmunology. Academic Press, 1981.

98. Riley V: Psychoneuroendocrine influences on immunocompetence and neoplasia. Science 212:1100, 1981.

99. Marx JL: The immune system "Belongs in the Body." Science 227:1190, 1985.

100. Takasugi N, Kotoo K, Fuwa T, Saito H: Effect of garlic on mice exposed to various stresses. Oyo Yakuri-Pharmacometrics 28:991, 1984.

101. Takasugi N, Kira K, Fuwa T: Effects of garlic extract preparation containing vitamins and ginseng-garlic preparation containing vitamin B1 on mice exposed

to stresses. Oyo Yakuri-Pharmacometrics 31:967, 1986.

102. Yokoyama K, Uda N, Takasugi N, Fuwa T: Anti-stress effects of garlic extract preparation containing vitamins and ginseng-garlic preparation containing vitamin B1 in mice. Oyo Yakuri-Pharmacometrics 31:977, 1986.

103. Saxena KK, Gupta B, Kulshrestha VK, Srivastava RK, Prasad DN: Effect of garlic pretreatment on isoprenaline-induced myocardial necrosis in albino rats. Indian J Physiol Pharmac 24:233, 1980.

104. Hiroshima University Group (G. Kajiyama): Clinical studies of Kyoleopin. Japanese J Clin Rep 16:1515, 1982.

105. Tanaka M: Clinical studies of Kyoleopin on complaints following treatment of gynecological malignancies. Japanese J New Remedies 31:1349, 1982.

106. Hasegawa Y, Kikuchi N, Kawashima Y, Ono Y, Shimizu K, Nishiyama M: Clinical effects of Kyoleopin against various complaints in the field of internal medicine. Japanese J New Remedies 32:365, 1983.

107. Cousins N: *Anatomy of an illness*. W.W. Norton & Co., Inc. New York, NY, 1979.

108. White EG: *Ministry of Healing*. Pacific Press, Mountain View, CA, 1905.

INDEX

ABOUT THE AUTHOR

Benjamin Lau, M.D., Ph.D. is a professor at California's Loma Linda University School of Medicine, where he has taught medical microbiology and immunology for more than fifteen years. He has several times been honored as "Teacher of the Year," and has been recognized as "Basic Science Investigator of the Year" for his research on cancer immunology. His interest in cancer immunology focuses on prevention and natural immunity. He and his associates have also been involved in garlic research for the past few years.

Dr. Lau received his M.D. degree from Loma Linda University and his Ph.D. in immunology from the University of Kentucky. He incorporates health education and lifestyle modification in his private practice, and is a sought-after speaker on the subjects of disease prevention and health promotion. This book is his response to patients and friends who were eager to learn the scientific evidence regarding garlic use.